Oh No! When a Parent Goes Away

By Dakota King-White, Ph.D.

Illustrated by Tyrus Goshay

Halo Publishing International

ISBN: 978-1-61244-628-8
Library of Congress Control Number: 2018900158

Printed in the United States of America

Halo Publishing International
1100 NW Loop 410
Suite 700 - 176
San Antonio, Texas 78213
Toll Free 1-877-705-9647
www.halopublishing.com
e-mail: contact@halopublishing.com

This book is dedicated to all the children around the world who have been impacted by parental incarceration.

Hi my name is Duane, and I am seven years old. Today I found out my dad went to jail. Oh no! What am I going to do? My dad is my friend, my best friend. Oh no! What am I going to do?

JOURNAL ENTRY

Who is your family member who is in jail?

Days have gone by and I found out that my dad is not coming home soon. I cried and screamed, "Please free my dad." Oh no! What am I going to do?

JOURNAL ENTRY

Who told you that your family member went to jail? What did you do when you found out?

Every day I think about my dad, and I wonder when I will see him and if I will talk to him soon. I often cry because I am sad and sometimes afraid. Oh no! What am I going to do?

JOURNAL ENTRY

How do you feel when you think about your family member
being in jail?

I am so frustrated that my dad is in jail. I asked my mom, "What am I going to do?" My mom decided to take me to see a lady called a "counselor." The counselor's name is Dr. D.

JOURNAL ENTRY

What do you do when you have uncomfortable feelings about your loved one being in jail?

My mom took me to see Dr. D, and during the first session I still had the question, "Oh no! What am I going to do?" Dr. D stated, "I am going to teach you coping strategies." I asked Dr. D, "What is coping?" She explained that coping is dealing with my problems or concerns in a healthy way.

JOURNAL ENTRY

Who do you talk to when you think about your family member who is in jail?

During my time with Dr. D, she plays games with me; she lets me draw pictures of my dad, and we talk about all the good times I had with him before he went to jail.

JOURNAL ENTRY

What are some activities you do when you start to think about your family member who is in jail?

The following week I went to see Dr. D. While meeting with her, she talked to me about how I was doing and asked me to talk about how I had been feeling since my dad was gone. I began to tell Dr. D about how I felt and that I was really sad that my dad was not coming home soon. While talking, I started to cry. Dr. D said, "It is okay to cry and to talk about your feelings." As I talked, I started to feel a little bit better. At the end of the session, Dr. D asked if it was okay for her to talk to my mother about what we had discussed. I said that it was fine.

My mom came into the counselor's office, and Dr. D told her about what we had talked about. My mommy started to cry. She said she never knew that I felt sad or afraid that my daddy was in jail.

JOURNAL ENTRY

Have you talked to your parent or caregiver about how you feel about your loved one being in jail? How does your parent or caregiver respond when you talk about your loved one who is in jail?

After we finished, my mom gave me a big hug and said that I can talk to her anytime when I am feeling sad or upset. That made me feel a lot better. After we left the counselor's office, my mom took me for ice cream, and she told me over and over again that she loved me and she cares so much about me.

JOURNAL ENTRY

Who are some people in your family or community you know who care about you?

The next week I went to see Dr. D, and she said, "Today we are going to journal about how you feel." I asked Dr. D, "What is a journal?" She explained that a journal is a safe place to write or draw about my thoughts and feelings. A journal sounded pretty cool. So Dr. D pulled out a piece of paper, and she told me to just begin to draw or write about how I was feeling. I started to draw a picture of a time my dad and I went to the park. We had so much fun at the park. Drawing the picture made me think about all the good times we spent together. I noticed that I had a huge smile on my face and that I had good memories of my dad. The memories didn't bring him back home, but they made me smile.

best Day Ever!

JOURNAL ENTRY

What positive memories do you have about your family member who is in jail?

After meeting with Dr. D, she told my mom that she wanted her to look for activities in my neighborhood that I could get involved in, like basketball, Boy Scouts, activities at my church or any other positive activity. My mommy thought that was a good idea and said she would look into it.

FIRST CAMPING TRIP!
PROUDMOM :) ♡

JOURNAL ENTRY

What are some activities you enjoy that you can get involved in at school or in the community?

During my last session with Dr. D, she explained that I was doing a lot better and that she was really proud of me. She asked me to tell her all the ways that I had learned to cope with my dad being gone. I was able to tell her five ways I had learned to cope:

1. I can talk about my feelings, and it is okay.
2. I can talk to a trusted adult like my mom or Dr. D.
3. I can journal about good times, bad times, or anything that comes to mind to help me deal with my dad being gone.
4. I can hang out with friends, family members, and others who love me.
5. I can get involved with activities that will make me a better person.

JOURNAL ENTRY

Write or draw five things you can do to help you cope while your loved one is in jail.

All these things did not bring my daddy back home right away, but they helped me to reach my goals and to cope. Thank you, Dr. D for helping me to deal with my daddy being gone.

About the Author

Dr. Dakota King-White has a Bachelor of Arts in Psychology, a Master of Arts in Counseling, and a Doctorate of Philosophy in Counselor Education and Supervision. She has done extensive research on the impact of parental incarceration on children and the psychological, emotional, and behavioral effects of incarceration. Through her research, she has designed a group counseling curriculum for the children of incarcerated parents, which has been implemented in K-12 education. She has also designed a mental health model that is used in K-12 education to help address the mental health needs of students within the academic setting. The model utilizes an interdisciplinary approach to address mental health needs within schools. Dr. King-White is passionate about children succeeding and believes that ALL children can succeed if given the right tools and opportunities.

www.ingramcontent.com/pod-product-compliance
Lightning Source LLC
Chambersburg PA
CBHW061416090426
42742CB00026B/3482